MANDALA

FULL PAGE ADULT COLORING BOOK

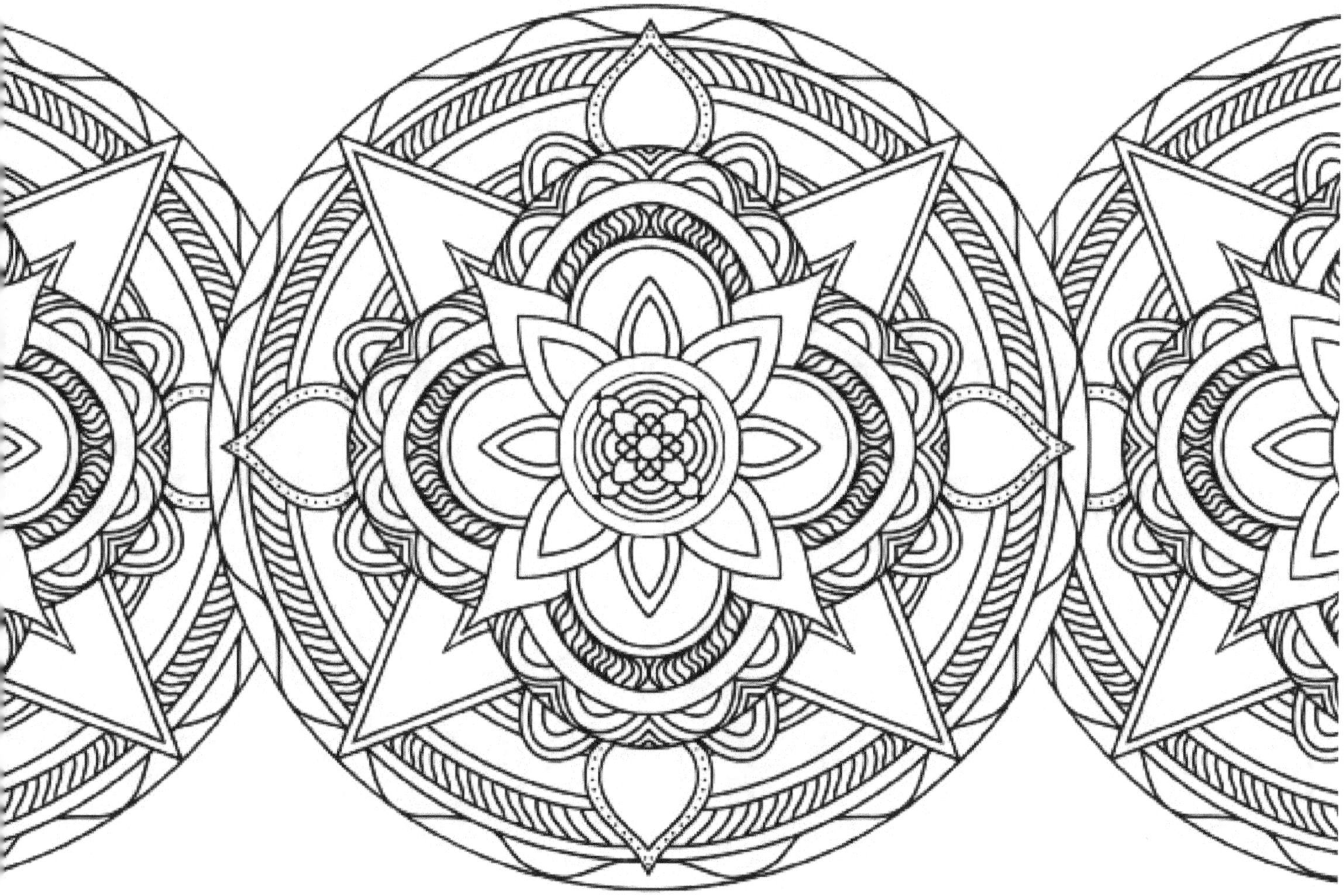

ELEVEN FLOWERS

PUBLISHING

COPYRIGHT 2020

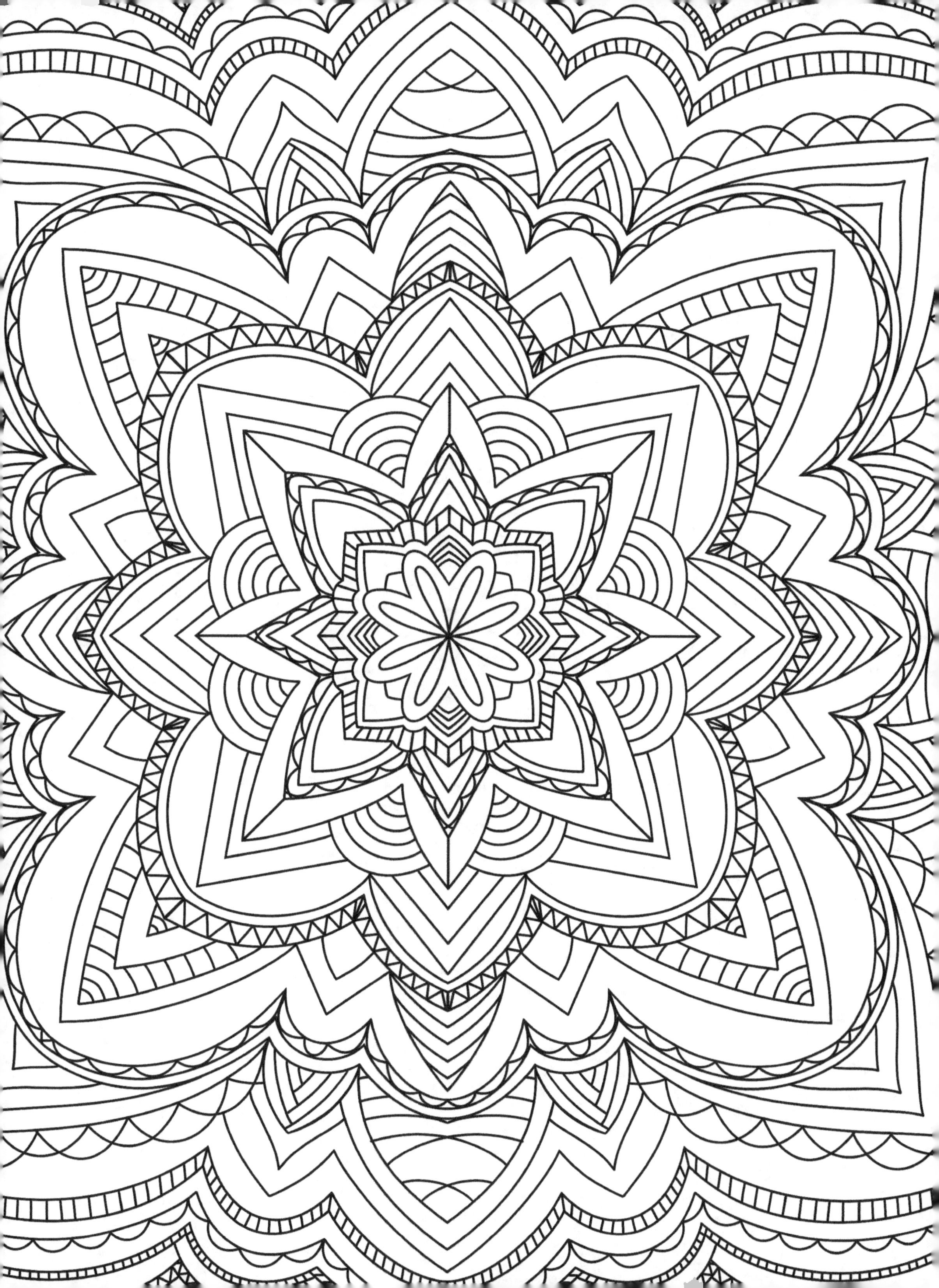

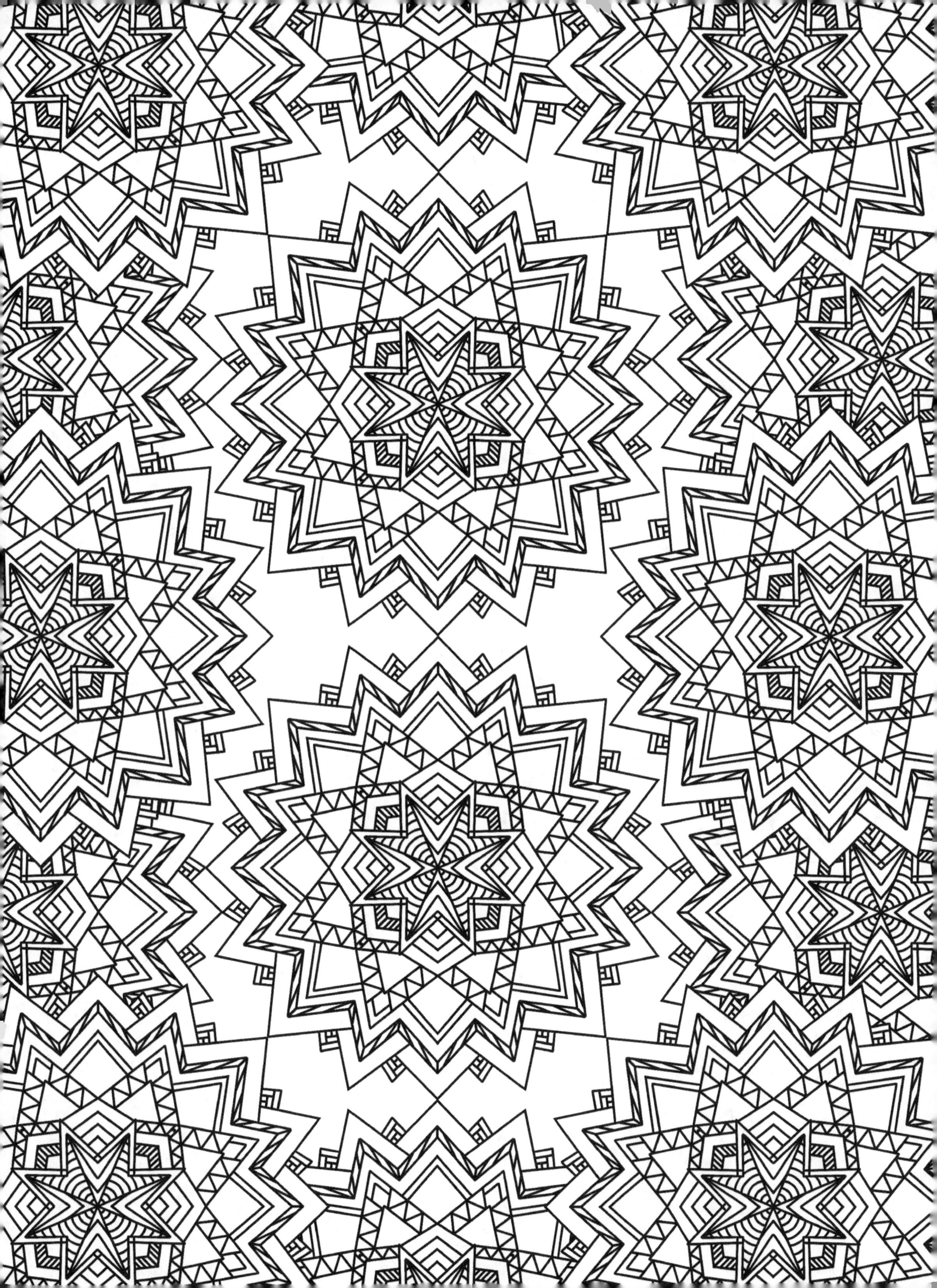

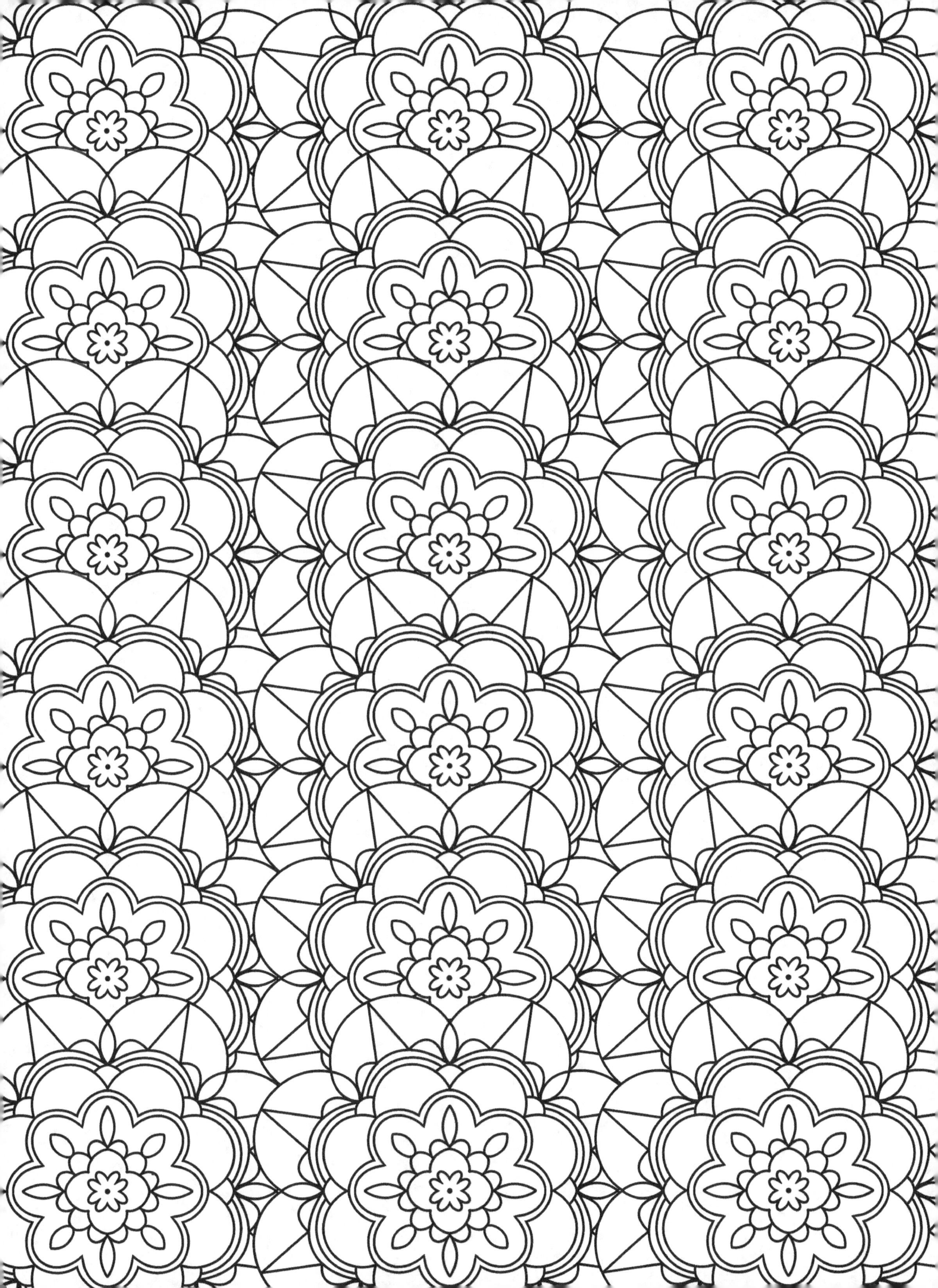

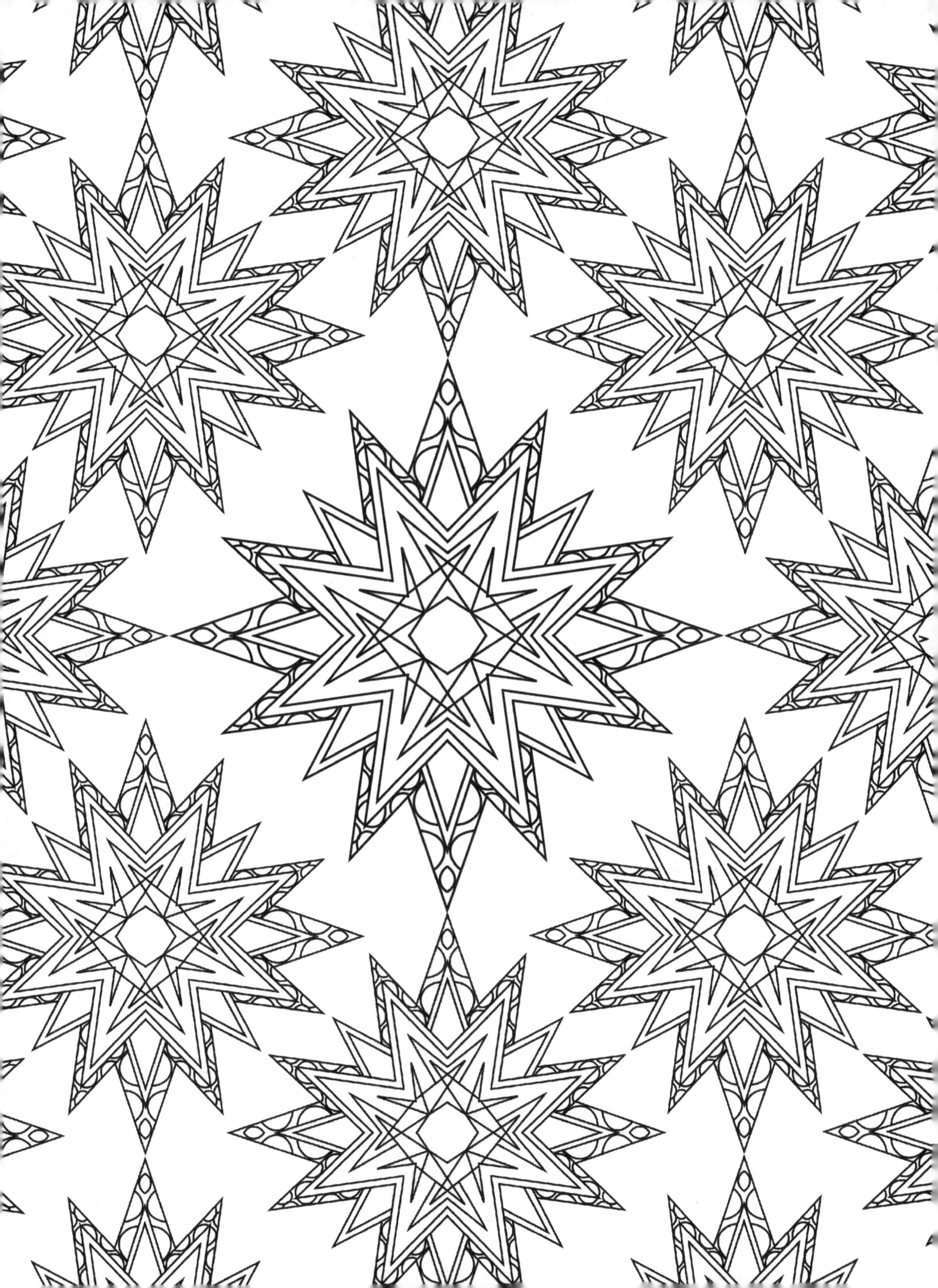

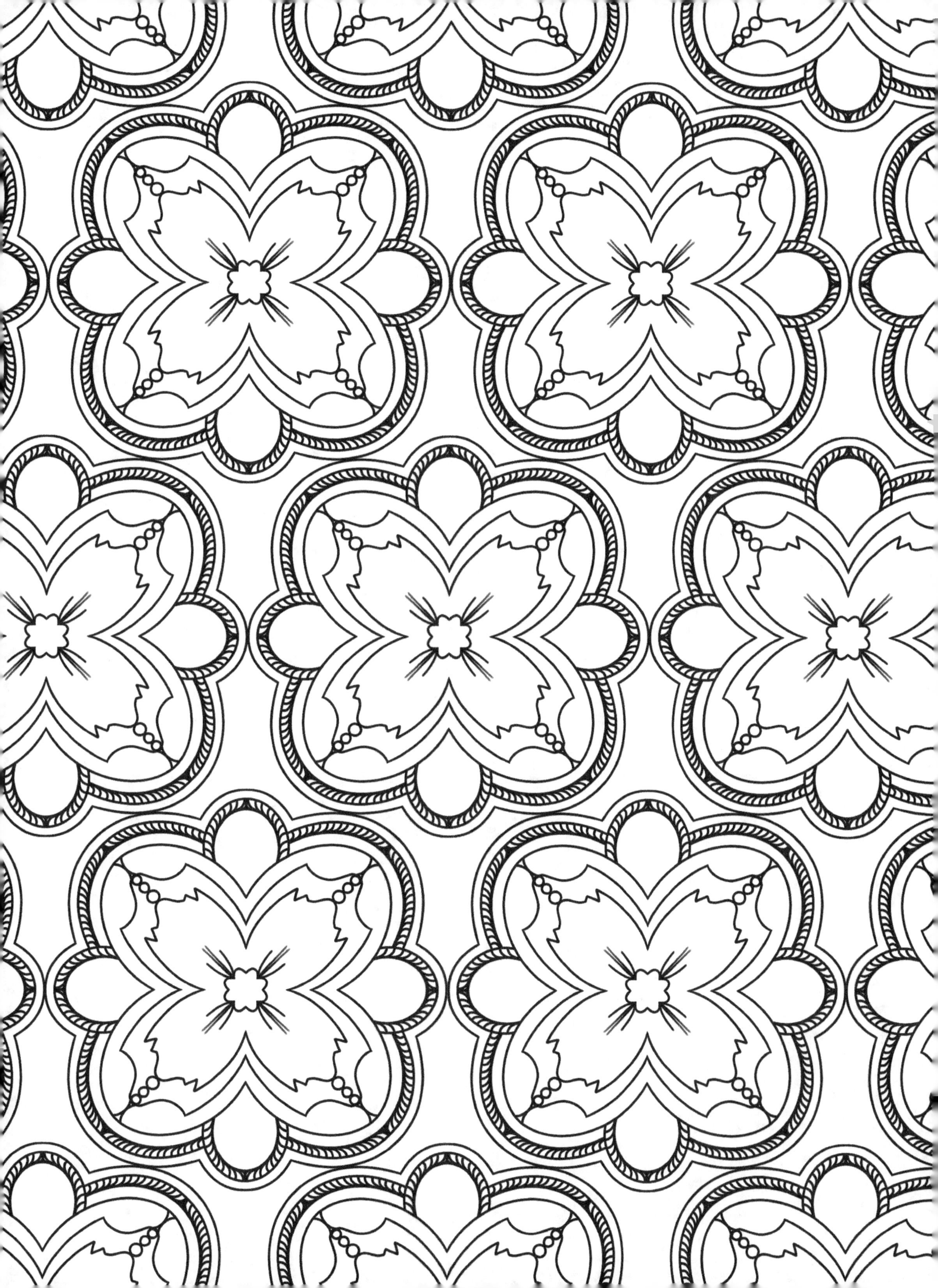

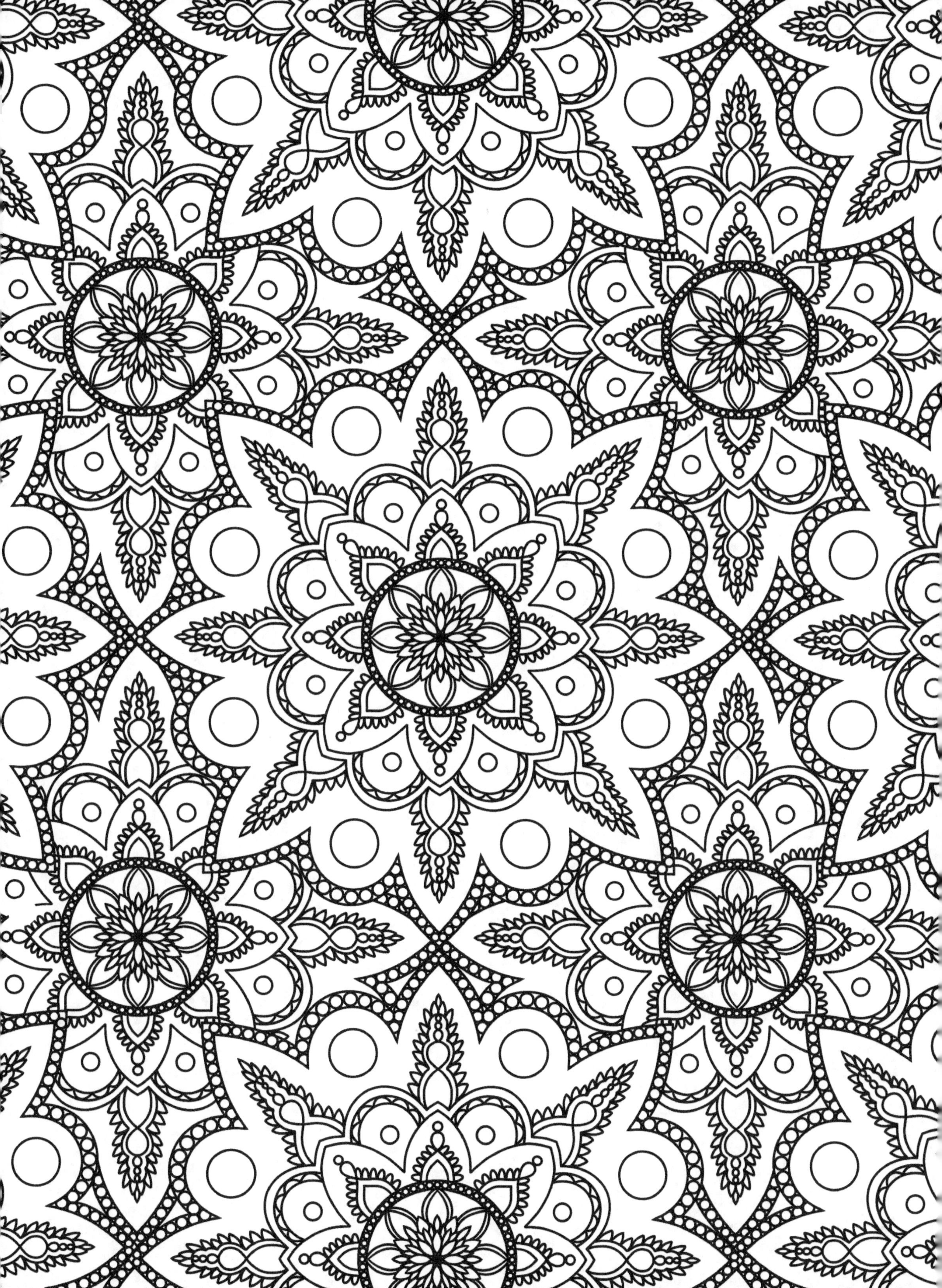

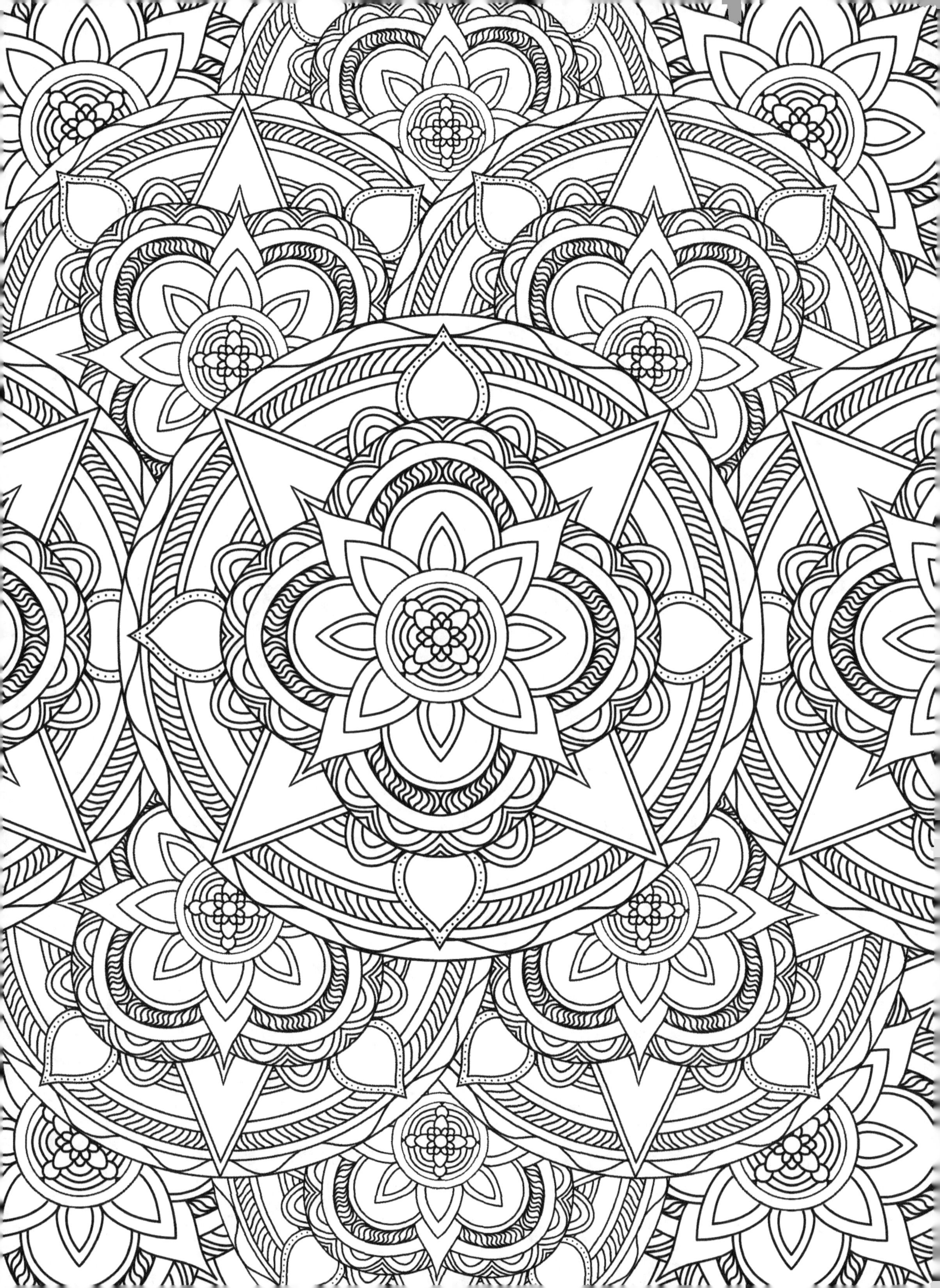

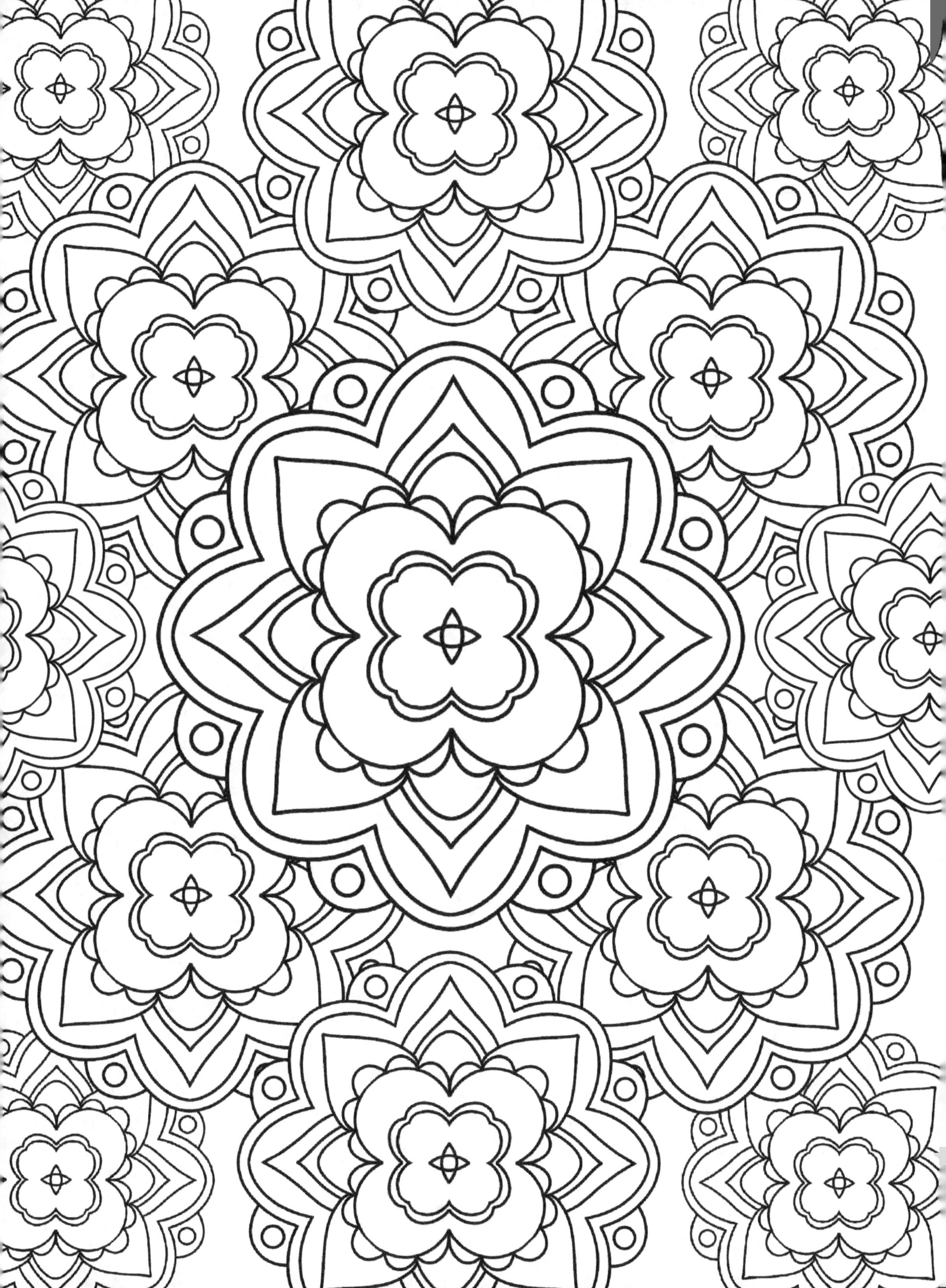

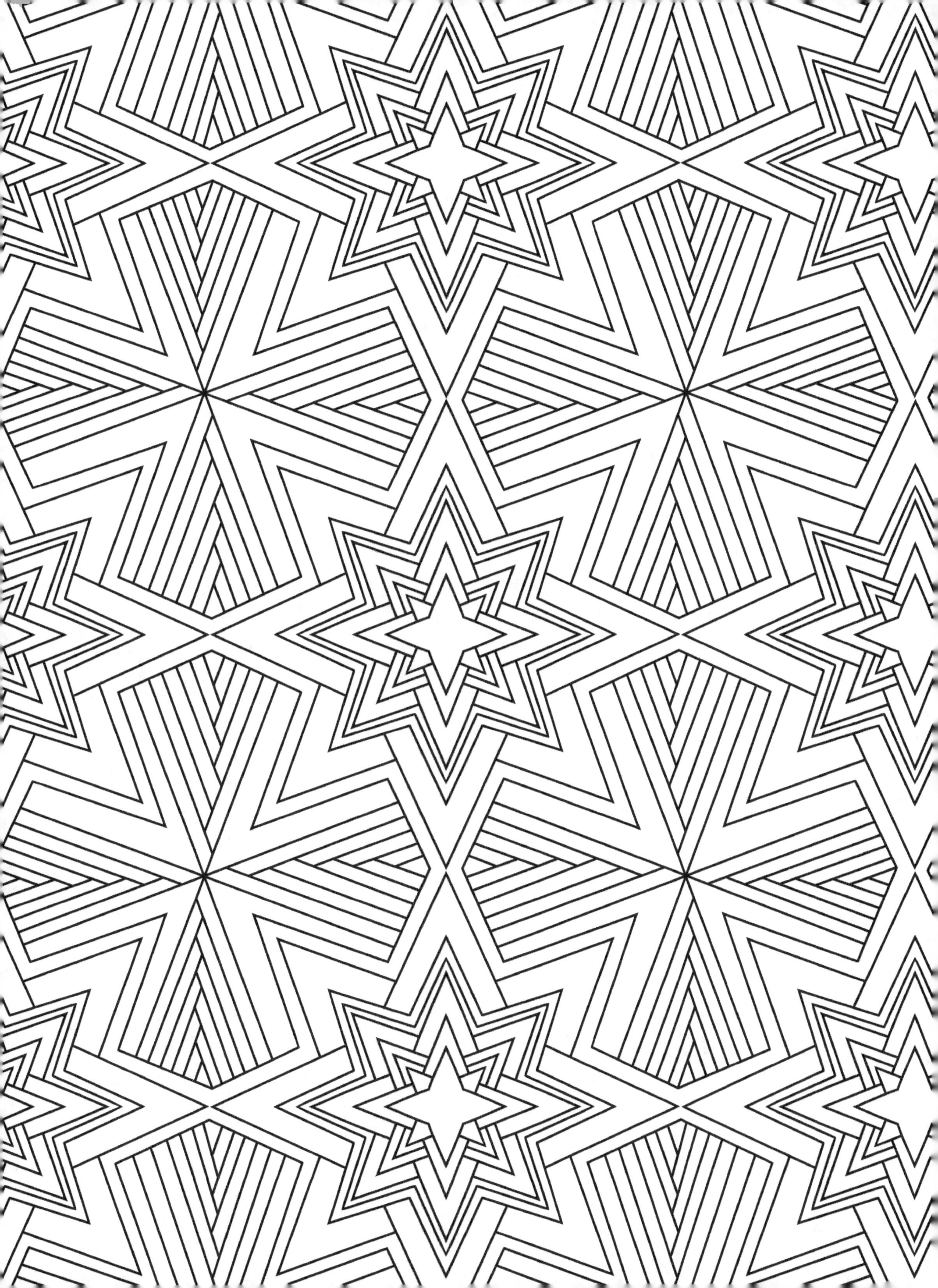

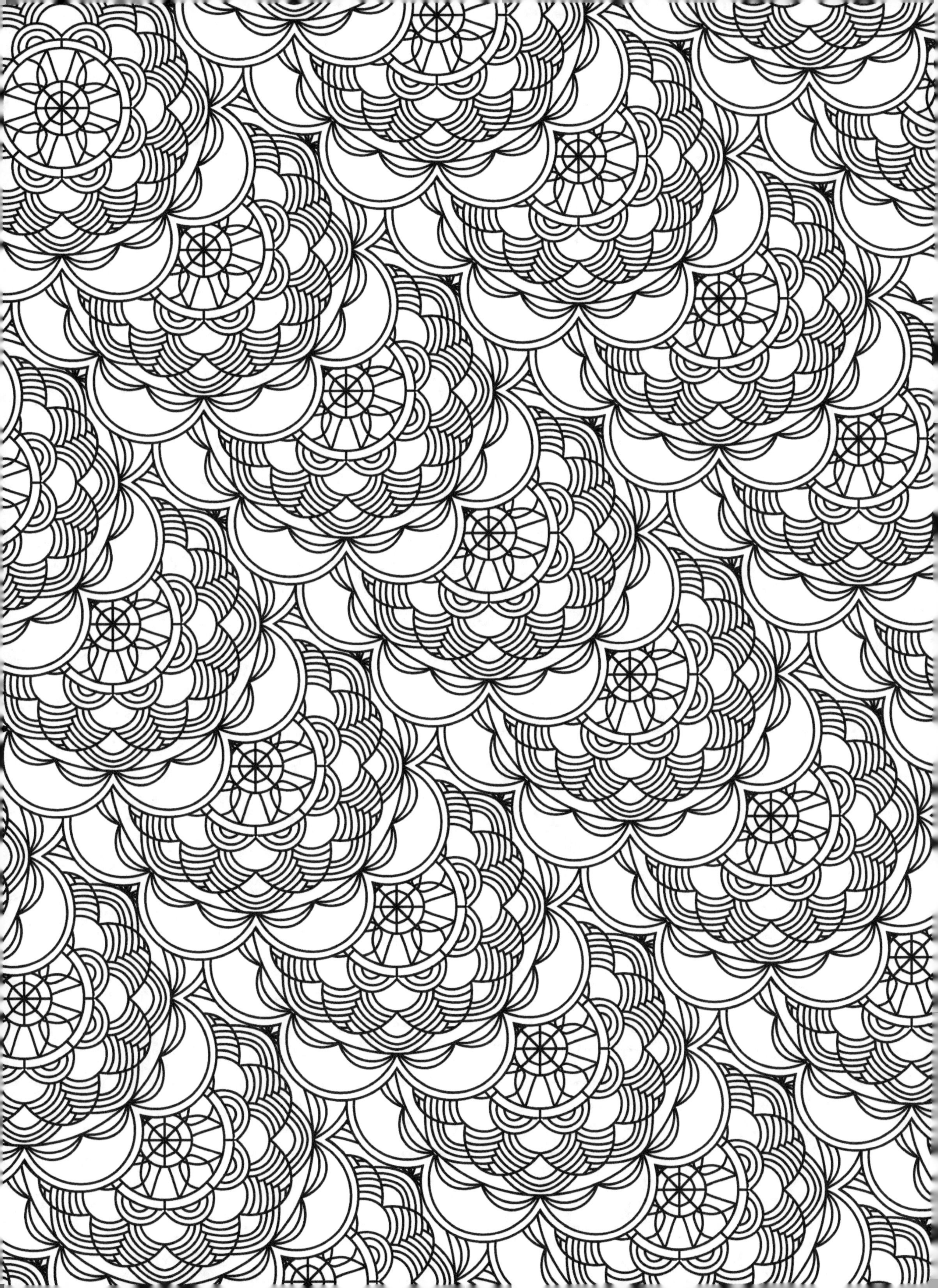

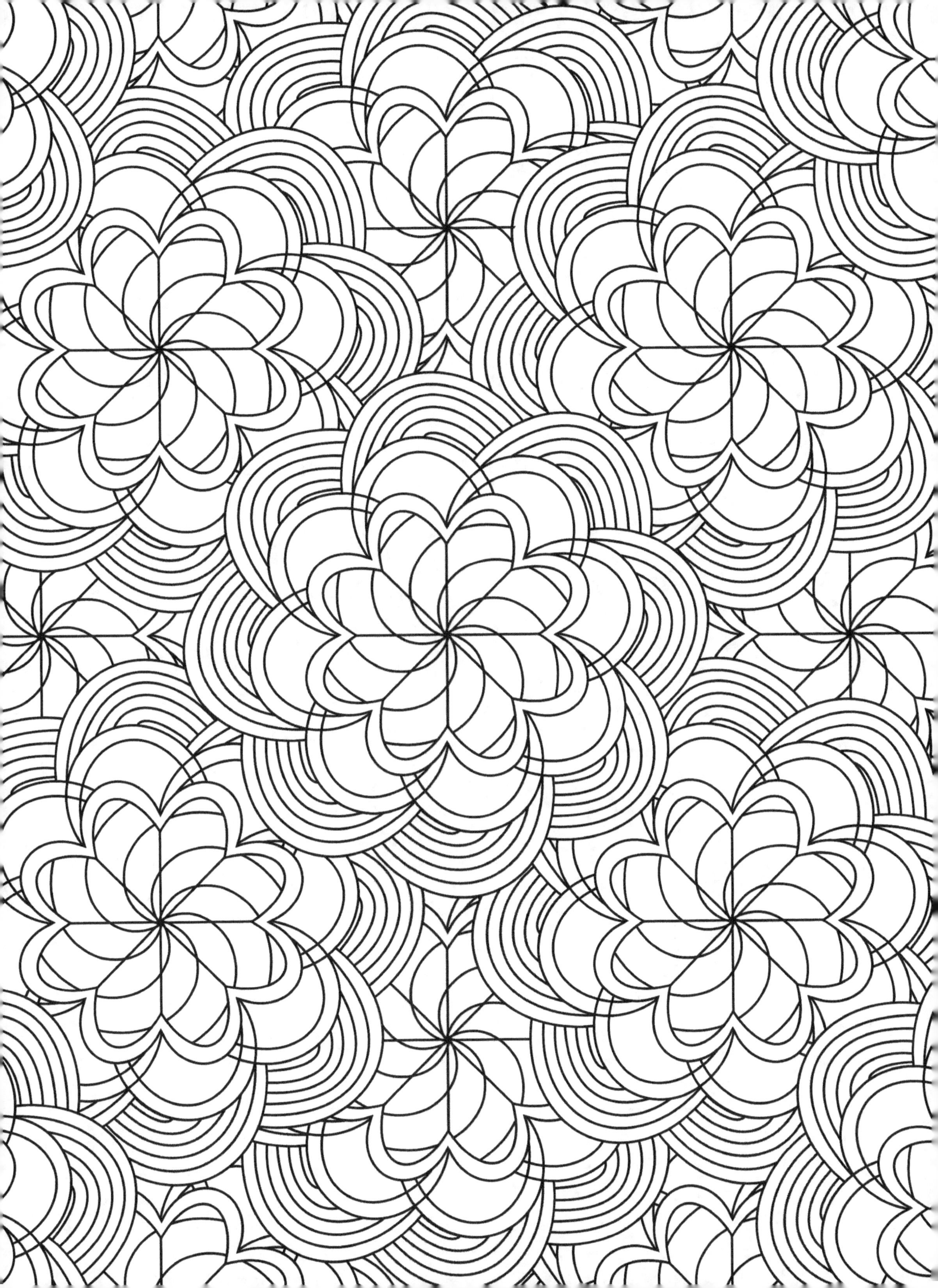

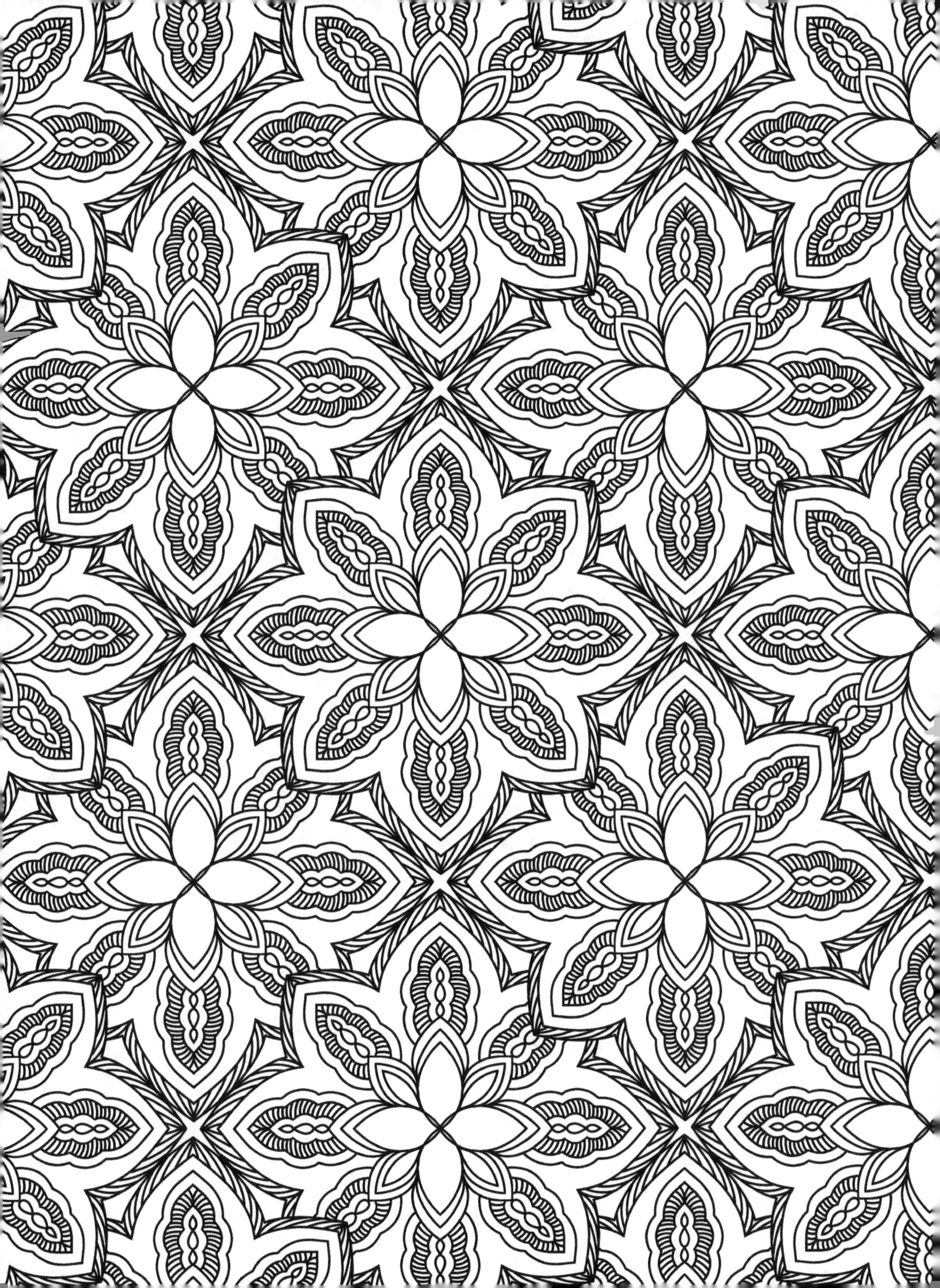

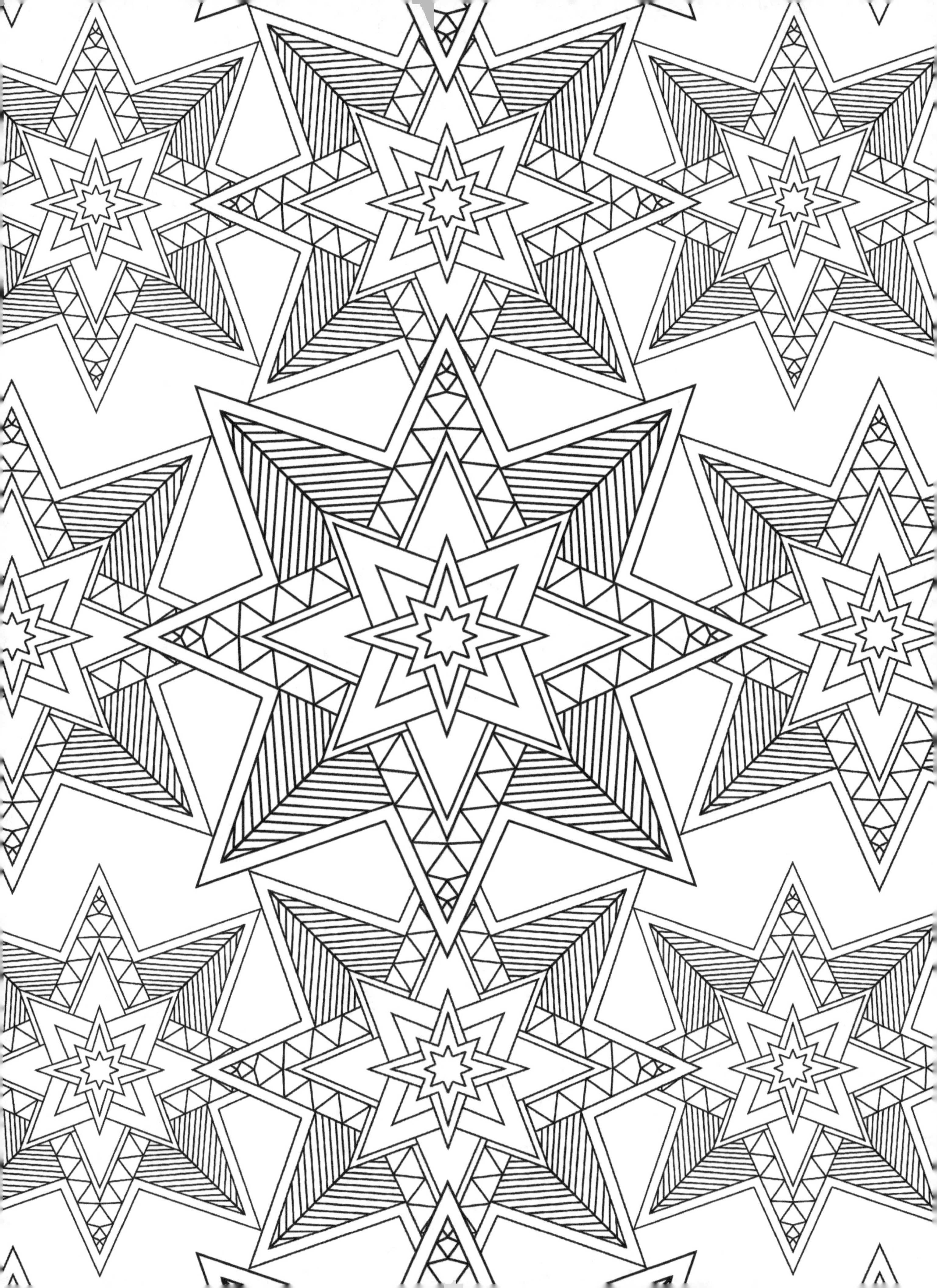

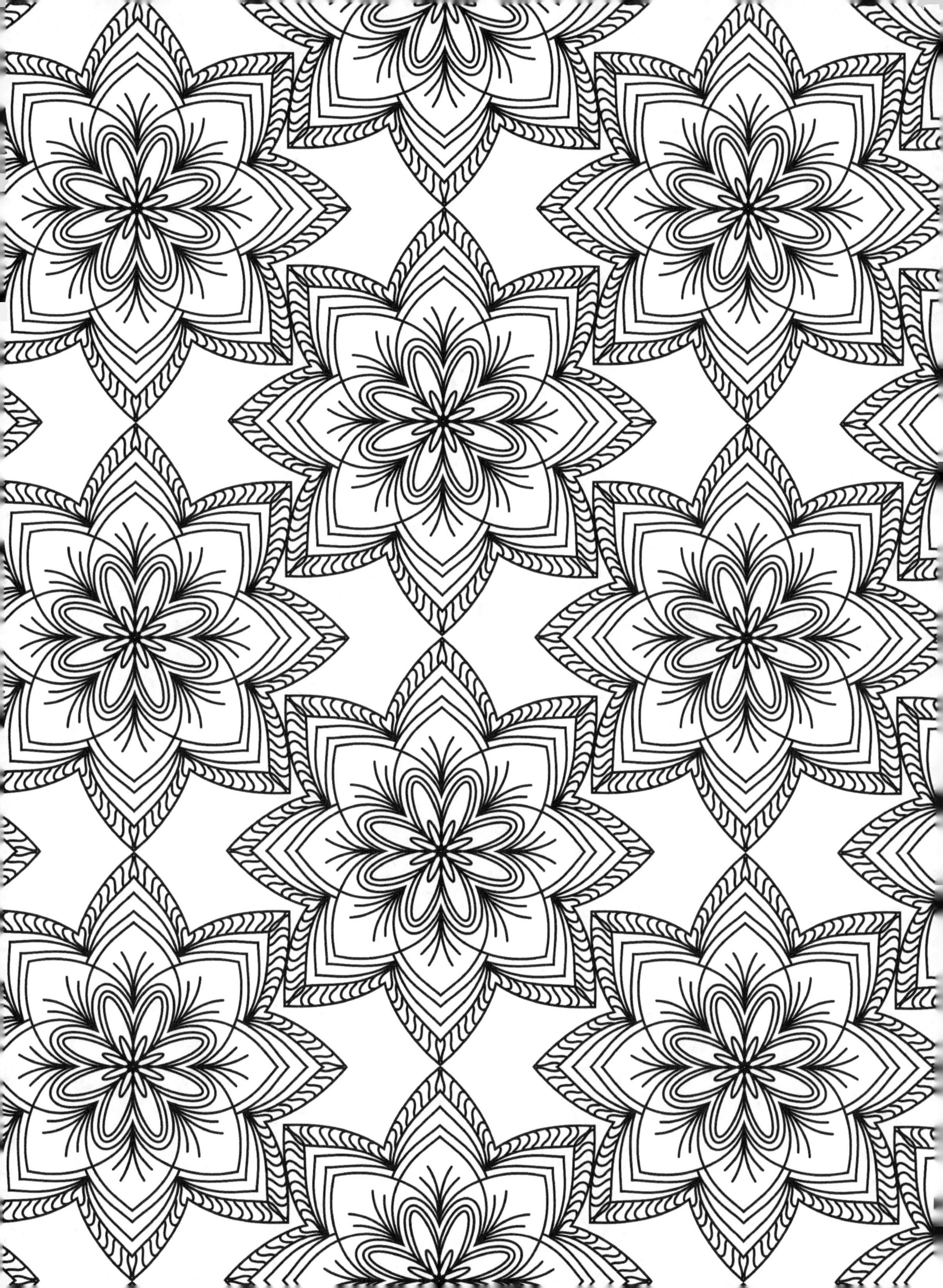

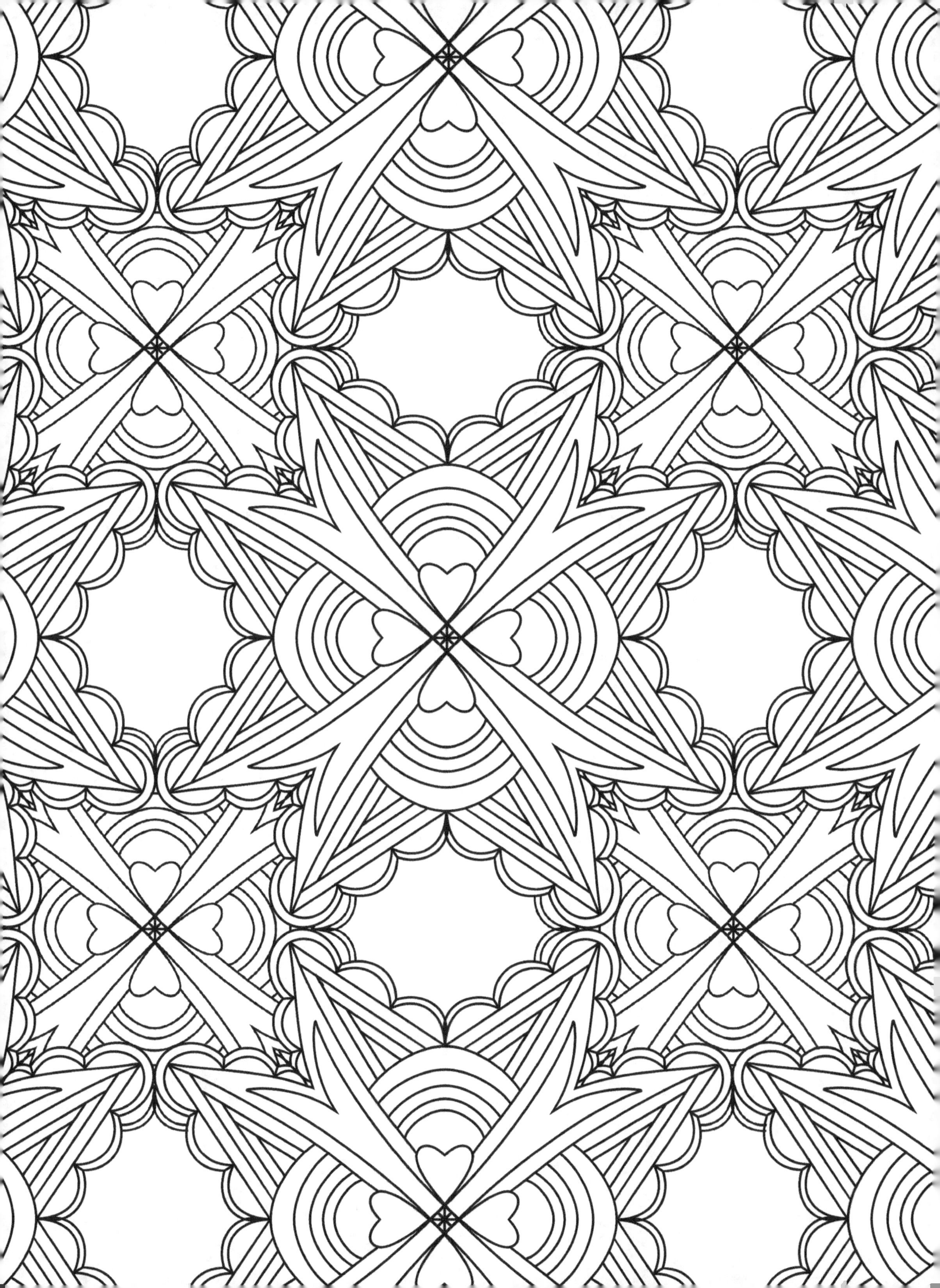

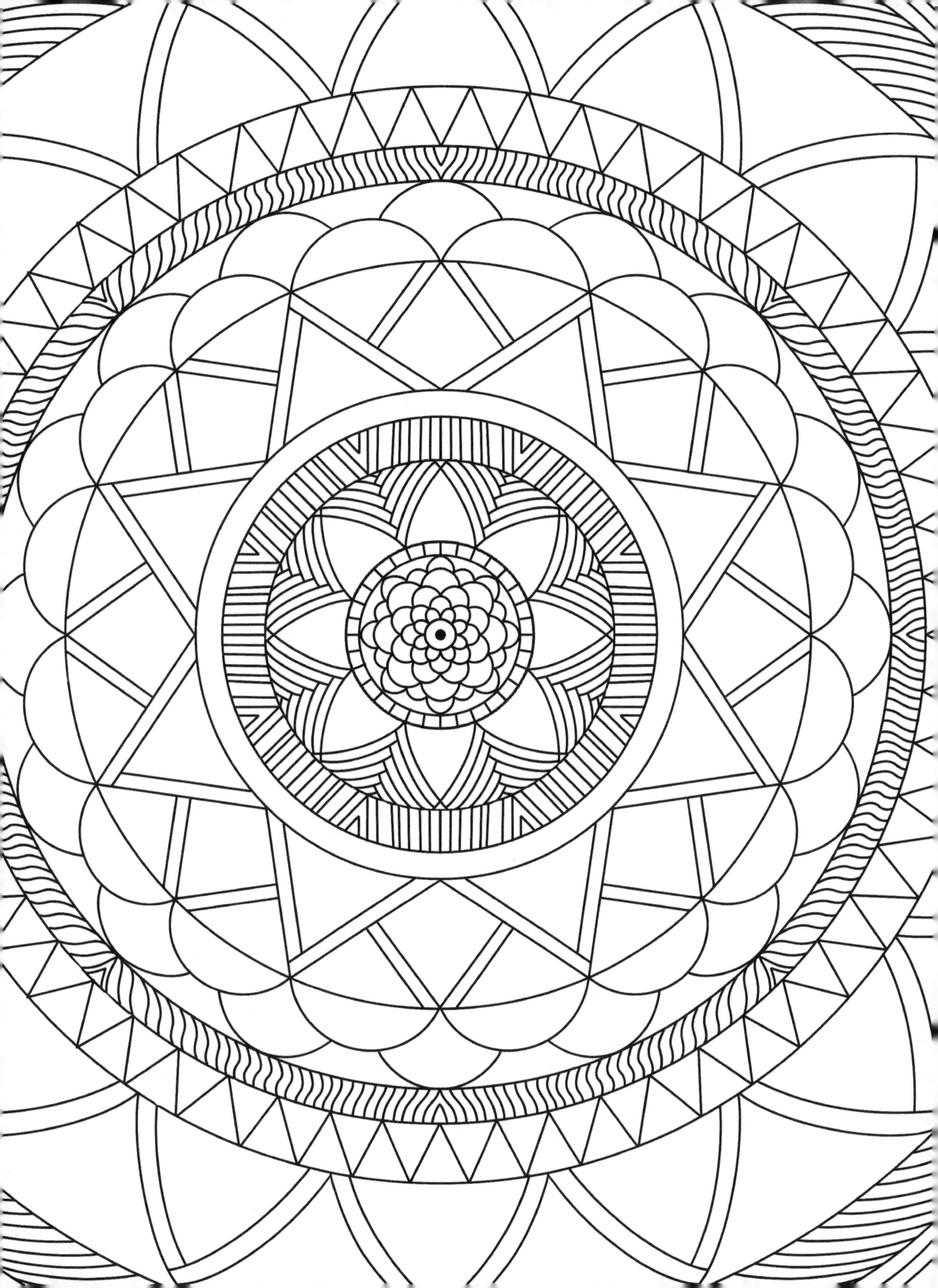

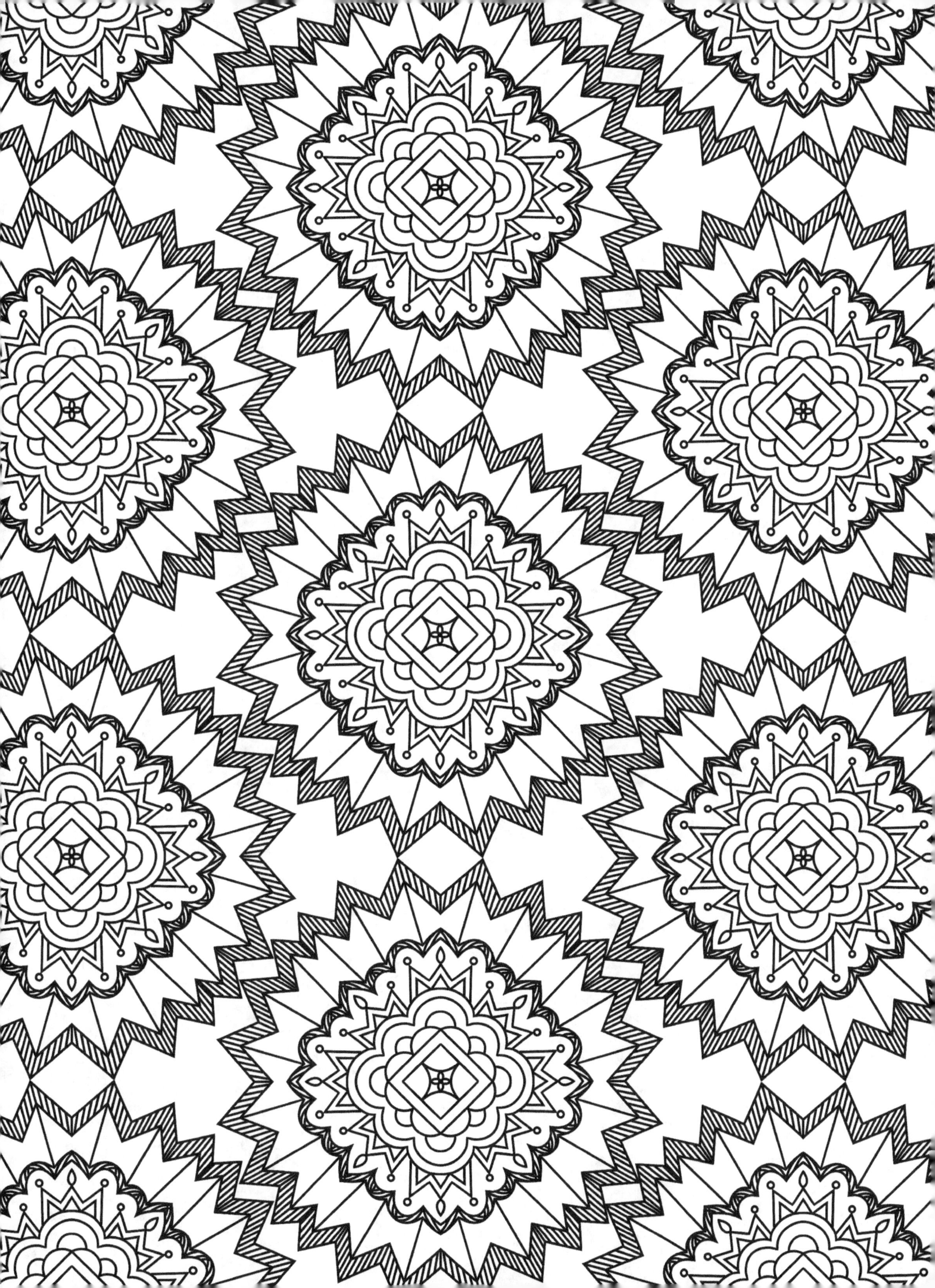

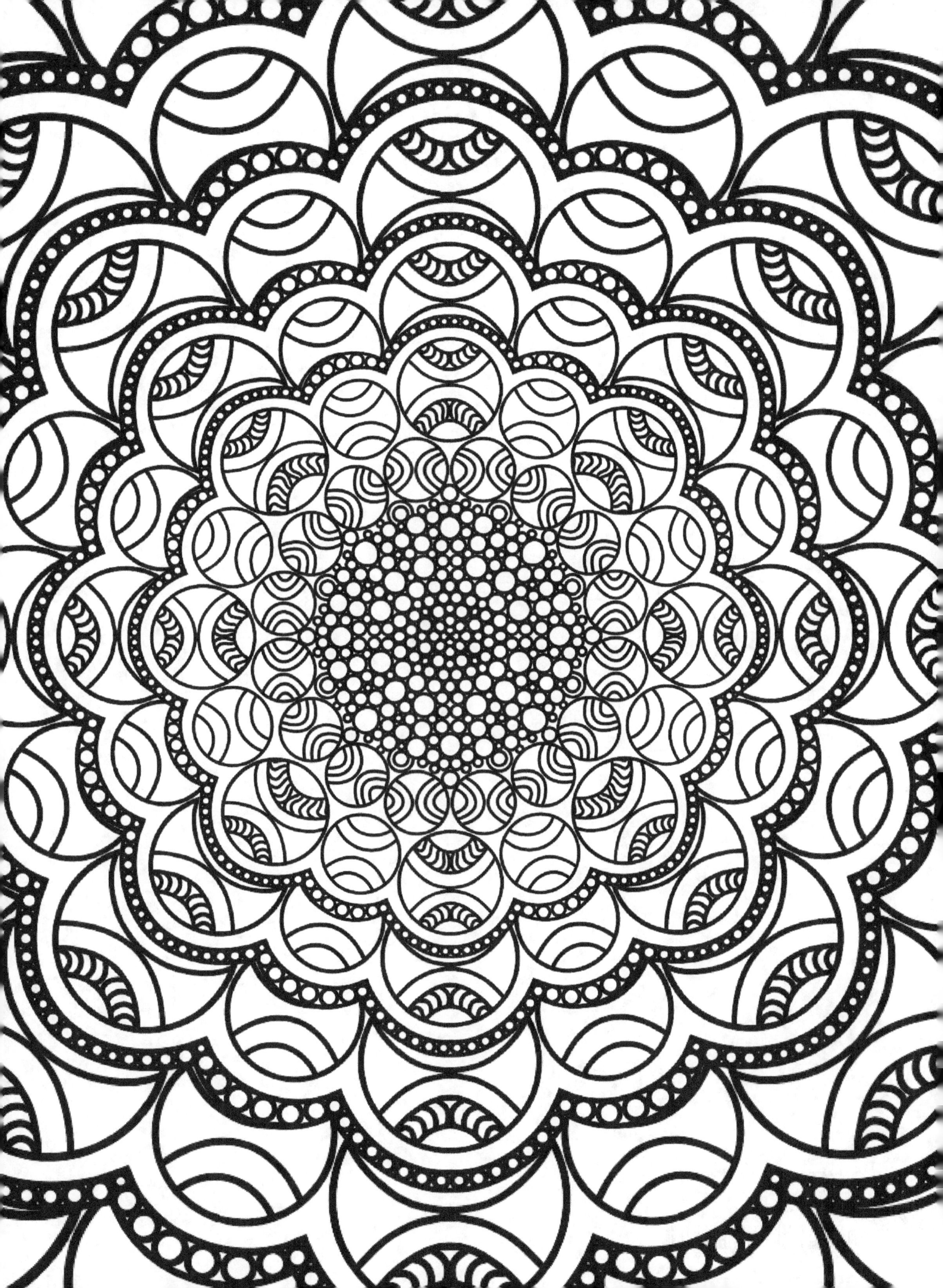

www.ingramcontent.com/pod-product-compliance
Lightning Source LLC
Chambersburg PA
CBHW081322250726
48662CB00008B/2700